ISBN 978-0-259-47762-4
PIBN 10818856

1 MONTH OF
FREE
READING

at
www.ForgottenBooks.com

By purchasing this book you are eligible for one month membership to ForgottenBooks.com, giving you unlimited access to our entire collection of over 1,000,000 titles via our web site and mobile apps.

To claim your free month visit:
www.forgottenbooks.com/free818856

The Glory of the Franciscan Order

What a Life!

WHAT A LIFE!

Ever heard of the Third Order o St. Francis? It is a youth movement Surprised? To convince yourself lool over the roster of its outstanding mem bers.

You will find it packed with youth ful faces. Of a bygone day there i St. Elizabeth of Hungary but 24 year old when she died. St. Louis of Japar 15, St. Rose of Viterbo 17, Bl. Mar Ann of Quito 27, St. Roch 32, and many more. The patron of the Thir Order, along with St. Elizabeth, is St Louis IX, King of France. He joine as a young prince and took to th battlefield for Christ. Hosts of othe saintly men and women, like S Conrad of Piacenza, joined as youn people—people who started young an had stayed with the Order.

Today's Third Order is equally rallying ground for young people w want to make something of themselv in God's way.

It was all started back about 7 years ago by a lad (pardon me, saint!) who discovered a new way life. St. Francis of Assisi began a sc of insurance company in which who joined and followed out the rul would have the best insurance possible —a guarantee of Heaven! But most important of all was the assurance that this was a most perfect way of life in the eyes of God.

Francis wanted happiness and gaiety. His followers were to go through life singing the praises of God. With the advent of Francis the common man learned what joy there was in knowing, loving, and serving God.

The world ran after Francis. Men gave up everything and left home to join him in his way of life. They took the vows of poverty, chastity and obedience, and became known as the First Order. Women followed, and Francis founded the Second Order for them. Finally, others with no call to community life with its vows, expressed the desire to become Franciscans also. St. Francis gave them a special rule of life, and these young men and women, and married men and women, form the widespread Third Order or the Order of Penance.

Hold on!

Don't shudder at the word "Penance." It's a word that from childhood has become a most dreaded expression, because of its association with spanking and sitting in a corner. But the Third Order does not apply that meaning to the word. All it asks are the things that Christ asks and the Church demands. It's all based on a policy of loving God and neighbor in an active way, rather than giving all one's time and talent to fun and money-making. This in turn calls for purity of mind and heart the poverty of moderation, and obedience to the will of God.

Would you like to promise, that for the rest of your life you will be pure of mind and heart, poor in spirit, and obedient? You hesitate. It is a big order. But you have a whole year to think it over during your year of probation. Then, too, don't forget other young people like yourself did it and are doing it. You can do it too.

Elinor Flynn of New York did it although she was a Broadway actress. The Third Order will fit as readily into your life. It is the way of moderation and "get-up."

Different? Yes.

"But," you say, "if there are no vows to take, and the rules are so simple, then it can't be any more im

Action Together

Third Order and Catholic Action

During recent years many zealous informed young Catholics have been ing the Catholic Action movement. T see the tremendous need for worker the vineyard of the Lord and have swered the call of the Church to sl in winning souls for Christ in the apostolate.

At the same time other young C olics, aware of the moral and relig deficiencies all around them, have centrated their efforts primarily upon own spiritual condition. Hearkening Christ's call to perfection, they have braced a way of life designed to en them to comply more fully with our ior's injunction. They have joined Third Order of St. Francis.

The complementary character of missions of the Catholic Action m ment and the Third Order is plainly ible. The former stresses action am others; the latter, action within one Neither can properly carry out its pose unless its members possess at l the spirit of the other. A Catholic Acti that would make no consistent effort self-improvement, would not succee converting others. Conversely, a T Order member that would confine spiritual labors to his own needs, w not be carrying out the full purpos the Third Order.

What, therefore, could be more fit

re beneficial to the cause of Christ
d the Church than that more Catholic
tionists actually join the Third Order,
d more Tertiaries enter the Catholic
tion movement? What could be more
keeping with the pronouncements of
Popes?

An Auxiliary

Pope Pius XI called the Third Order
most valuable and providential aux-
ry of Catholic Action (cf. Osservatore
mano, Oct. 12, 1938). And rightly so.
e Third Order rule covers the Catholic
tion Program — and more. The Third
der is, in reality, a school of thorough
tholicism, of perfect Gospel life after
manner compatible with secular life;
s the heart of the interior life and of
apostolate.

As is well known, the Third Order
ves to realize a twofold purpose; Pri-
rily personal sanctification, and sec-
larily the apostolate.

As to personal sanctification, the Third
der educates its members to greater
fection. It achieves this aim by giving
m a methodical and progressive train-
in the principles and benefits of con-
it life. It supplies them furthermore
h special means to the end in the form
a practical rule of perfection. Thus it
vides for the Catholic Actionist's per-
al spiritual development — which is
natter even more vital to him than his
ostolate.

This very thought was expressed Archbishop Joseph Charbonneau Montreal at a Catholic Action congre in Montreal in the fall of 1945. He sa "Some associations have as their p mary objective the sanctification of t faithful. Such are the Third Orders; the associations are prior to and fundamen to Catholic Action. I wish, therefore, tl all members of the Catholic Action mo' ments enter such associations. On t other hand, Tertiaries should consic it their duty to participate actively in t work of Catholic Action."

Thus it is that, through sympathe understanding and active cooperatic these instruments of God collaborate w one another and help one another spre the spirit of the Gospel in society.

In the United States the Third Orc of St. Francis has an Episcopal Protec in the person of Archbishop Cushing Boston. He represents the Third Orc officially at the meetings of the Hierarc of the United States. Due to this measu not only has the Third Order of St. Frc cis a direct mandate for auxiliary Catl lic Action from the Holy See (cf. Tertii Franciscalium as above, and Sacra P pediem of Benedict XV, Jan. 6, 192 but the Hierarchy of our country exten to our National Tertiary Organizati its special formal recognition as a loca mandated auxiliary force of Cathc Action.

model for the activity of our modern
men in Catholic Action is St. Fran-
— his life and his virtues as well as
work — the thorough practice of the
spel, public profession of the Faith,
spirit of poverty, the exercise of
rity, intervention in favor of the under-
vileged, obedience to the Holy See,
erence for bishops and priests, whom
mcis called his masters, and the or-
nization of the laity for holy purposes.
he popes of our day have very in-
ently emphasized the need of spread-
the Third Order, making it, as it were,
backbone of Catholic Action and the
ool in which the spirit of its mem-
s should be formed. That is due to the
ll and virile strength of the Third Order,
nded as it is on the Gospel and on
rough-going Catholicism. It is also due
he fact that the Third Order is a way
life easily adaptable to all conditions
l walks of life — without distinction
to age or sex.

tholic Action into Third Order—
rtiaries into Catholic Action

a becoming fervent Tertiaries, Catho-
Action members will respond more
y to their vocation as efficient and ac-
nplished lay apostles. On the other
ld, by joining actively in the Catholic
ion movement, Tertiaries will comply
re completely with the secondary pur-
e of the Third Order and become lead-
in Catholic Action.

To be convinced of this aim of
Third Order, one need only examine
following points of the rule of the Th
Order: the requirements of admission,
novitiate, the wearing of the habit,
rule of moderation enjoined, the regu
reception of the sacraments, daily M
when possible, the recitation of the do
office, the examination of conscience,
avoidance of profanity, and above
the public profession to strive towc
perfection — a profession officially
cepted by Mother Church.

As regards the apostolate, or exte
action, the rule of the Third Order is
perfect agreement with the statutes
Catholic Action in such points as (cf. '
tium Franciscalium, Pius X, Sept. 8, 19

Profession and spreading of the fo
especially by means of the catech
and the campaign against blasphem
and obscene language (Rule: 1-1, 2-

The campaign against indecent fo
ions, against luxury, dangerous dan
suggestive plays; for the organizatior
leisure (Rule: 2-1).

Temperance in eating and drink
and, therefore, campaigning for tem
ance and abstinence movements (R
2-3).

Wholesome reading, campaign aga
corrupt literature, spreading of good re
ing material (Rule: 2-8).

The spirit of fraternity, of family life,
ucation of children along this line (R
1-2, 2-8).

he spirit of harmony, of benevolence,
oy and of mutual charity; wherefore,
peacemaking role of the Tertiary, and
care to avoid lawsuits (Rule: Ch. 2-9).
he duty of making a will, and there-
family thrift, the spirit of poverty with
iew to charity, union with God and
coring of the needy (Rule: 2-1 and 7).
isiting the sick and solicitude to secure
them the blessings of the last Sacra-
nts (Rule: 2-13).
pecial attention given to the deceased
le: 2-14).
evotion to all good works, care for
needy, maintenance of poor churches
l, therefore, setting aside of the com-
n fund, assistance in the works of
erdotal, religious and missionary
ations (Rule: 2-8 and 12).
is impossible here to recall the his-
r of seven centuries, but it is not an
ggeration to say that all the activities
rocated today by Catholic Action
e been favorite pursuits of the Third
ler in the course of the past centuries.
uch is the program of the apostolate
he Third Order.
ardinal Bertram of Germany, Arch-
nop of Breslau, Franciscan Tertiary,
rightly pronounced these judicious
ds (address, 1930):
Saint Francis holding up the walls of
Lateran basilica appears to me as
forerunner of modern Catholic Action.
spent all his strength to restore the
ily and Catholic morals, to re-Christ-

ianize the nations of the world; in a
word, he strove to realize the progr
which Catholic Action endeavors to
fill."

Catholic Action Patron
Third Order Foun

The parallel between the activities
Catholic Action and of the Third Or
helps us to understand better the moti
which led Pope Benedict XV to name c
Pope Pius XI to confirm Saint Francis
the Patron of Catholic Action (cf. Rite
piatis, Oct. 4, 1927). According to Po
Pius XI, the title of patron does not im
only the idea of an intercessor, but mai
that of a model to imitate. That is w.
Osservatore Romano wrote in 19
"When the Holy See chooses a saint
a protector for a certain kind of work,
is not meant to be a mere intercess
honored with a vain title to which nd
ing corresponds in reality. . . ."

Saint Theresa of the Child Jesus 1
been proclaimed the patron saint of
foreign missions; the Cure' of Ars, t
of the parochial clergy; Saint Pasc.
Baylon, of Eucharistic congresses c
societies; St. Thomas Aquinas, of stud
youth; Saint Vincent de Paul, of all wo
of charity. These patrons were carefu
selected because their lives were
dorned with those particular virtues wh
must be practiced by those who
placed under their patronage.

One may, therefore, rightly say t

Catechism 4096B
of the Third Order
# of St. Francis

By Fr. Ferdinand Gruen, O. F. M.

Whoever shall follow this rule,
peace on them and mercy."
Gal. vi, 16

Eighteenth Edition
Printed in U. S. A.

FRANCISCAN HERALD PRESS
1434 West 51st Street
CHICAGO, ILL.
1943

FOREWORD

THE following pages contain an explanation, in question and answer form, of the Rule of the Third Order of St. Francis, as modified by Pope Leo XIII. The booklet has proved so popular with American Tertiaries that edition after edition has become necessary. Since former editions have been officially adopted in many Third Order fraternities, it has been deemed advisable to make no material changes in subsequent editions. The author is happy to think that his little work has been helpful to Directors as well as Tertiaries, and he takes this occasion to thank them for the kind reception they have given it. He wishes also to express his indebtedness to Fr. Eugene d'Oisy, O. F. M. Cap., of whose *Catechisme ou Petit Manuel* the present booklet is largely an adaptation.

24,935.

Nihil Obstat,
Fr. Jacobus Meyer, O. F. M.
Censo

Imprimatur,
Fr. Vincent Schrempp, O. F. M.
Minister

Imprimatur,
†Georgius Card. Mundelein
Archiepiscopus

RULE OF THE THIRD ORDER SECULAR OF ST. FRANCIS

CHAPTER I

Reception, Novitiate and Profession

1. Only those may be received as members who have completed their fourteenth year, and are of good character, peace-loving, and above all of tried fidelity in the practice of the Catholic Faith and in loyalty to the Roman Church and the Apostolic See.

2. Married women may not be received without the husband's knowledge and consent, unless their confessor judges otherwise.

3. The members shall wear the small scapular and the cord as prescribed; if they do not, they deprive themselves of the rights and privileges of the Order.

4. All who enter the Order must pass the first year in probation; then they shall duly make their profession upon the Rule of the Order, pledging themselves to observe the Commandments of God and of the Church, and to render satisfaction if they have failed against their profession.

CHAPTER II

Rule of Life

1. In all things let the members of the Third Order avoid extremes of cost and style, observing the golden mean suited to each one's station in life.

2. Let them with the utmost caution keep away from dances and shows which savor of license; as well as from all forms of dissipation.

3. Let them be temperate in eating and drinking, and devoutly say grace before and after meals.

4. They shall fast on the vigil of the Immaculate Conception and on that of St. Francis; they are to be highly commended who, according to the original Rule of the Tertiaries, also either fast on Fridays or abstain from fleshmeat on Wednesdays.

5. They shall approach the Sacraments of Penance and of the Holy Eucharist every month.

6. Tertiaries among the clergy, since they recite the Divine Office daily, shall be under no further obligation in this regard. Lay members who recite neither the Canonical Hours, nor the Little Office of the Blessed Virgin Mary, shall say daily twelve Our Fathers, Hail Marys and Glorys, unless they are prevented by ill health.

7. Let those who are entitled to make a last will and testament, do so in good time.

8. In their daily life let them strive to lead others by good example and to promote practices of piety and good works. Let them not allow books or publications which are a menace to virtue, to be brought into their homes, or to be read by those under their care.

9. Let them earnestly maintain the spirit of charity among themselves and towards others. Let them strive to heal discord wherever they can.

10. Let them never take an oath except when necessary. Let them never use indecent language or vulgar jokes. Let them examine their conscience every night whether they have offended in this regard; if they have, let them repent and correct the fault.

11. Let those who can do so, attend Mass every day. Let them attend the monthly meetings called by the Prefect.

12. Let them contribute according to their means to a common fund, from which the poorer members may be aided, especially in time of sickness, or provision may be made for the dignity of Divine Worship.

13. Let the officers either personally visit a sick member, or send some one to perform the services of charity. In case of serious illness let them remind and urge the sick person to arrange in time the affairs of his soul.

14. At the funeral of a deceased member the resident and visiting Tertiaries shall assemble and say in common five decades of the Rosary for the soul of the departed. Moreover, let the priests at the Holy Sacrifice and the lay members, if possible, having received Holy Communion, pray with fervent charity for the eternal rest of the deceased.

CHAPTER III

Offices, Visitation, and the Rule Itself

1. The offices shall be conferred at a meeting of the members. The term of these offices shall be three years. Let no one without good reason refuse an office tendered him, and let no one discharge his office negligently.

2. The Visitor, who is charged with the supervision of the Order, shall diligently investigate whether the Rule is properly observed. Therefore, it shall be his duty to visit the Fraternities every year, or oftener if need be, and hold a meeting, to which all the officers and members shall be summoned. Should the Visitor recall a member to his duty by admonition or command, or impose a salutary penance, let such member meekly accept the correction and not refuse to perform the penance.

3. The Visitors are to be chosen from the First Franciscan Order or from the Third Order Regular, and

shall be appointed by the provincial or local superiors when requested. Laymen cannot hold the office of Visitor.

4. Disobedient and harmful members shall be admonished of their duty a second and a third time; if they do not submit, let them be dismissed from the Order.

5. Those who offend against any provision of this Rule, do not incur the guilt of sin unless in so doing they also transgress the Commandments of God or of the Church.

6. Should a just and serious cause prevent a member from observing any provision of the Rule, such person may be dispensed therefrom, or the regulation may be prudently commuted. For this purpose the ordinary superiors of the First and Third Order Regular, as also the aforesaid Visitors, shall have full power.

THIRD ORDER

CHAPTER I
St. Francis and His Orders

1. Who is Saint Francis of Assisi?

St. Francis of Assisi is the illustrious founder of three great religious orders: the Order of Friars Minor, the Order of Poor Clares, and the Third Order.

2. Which are the principal traits of his character?

St. Francis was a man of lofty ideals, chivalrous sentiments, and great strength of character; a man thoroughly "Catholic and wholly apostolic," entirely devoted to the Church and to the salvation of souls. He is frequently called the poor, the humble, or the seraphic Francis.

3. By what means did he attain to sanctity?

By his profound and childlike piety, which led him to an intimate union with God, and filled him with a burning zeal for God's glory and the welfare of men.

11

4. Which were his favorite devotions?

St. Francis was particularly devoted to the mysteries of the life of our Savior and of his Blessed Mother, most especially, to the Blessed Eucharist.

5. What was the mission assigned him by God?

His mission was, to bring about in the world a revival of Christian ideals by the imitation of our Savior's life and virtues.

6. What influence did he exert on society?

He became the reformer of Christian life and morals in the thirteenth century. The impression he left on his own and on succeeding ages, was deep and lasting, his influence making itself felt even to the present day.

7. Which is the first order founded by St. Francis?

It is the Order of Friars Minor or Lesser Brethren, which is divided into three families, namely, the Franciscans, the Conventuals, and the Capuchins.

8. Which is the second order founded by St. Francis?

The second order is that of the Poor Ladies or Poor Clares, whose aim it is to work for the salvation of souls by prayer and penance. It is divided into divers observances.

9. Which is the third order founded by St. Francis?

It is the Order of Penance, also called simply the Third Order.

12

11. How are the members of the Third Order Secular called?

They are called Brethren of Penance or Franciscan Tertiaries.

12. What does the name "Franciscan Tertiaries" signify?

It signifies "of or belonging to the Third Order Secular of St Francis."

CHAPTER II
The Third Order of St. Fran

13. How many Third Orders are there?

There are eight Third Orders, which differ
one another in name and form, according to
respective affiliation with one or the other
religious Orders of Franciscans, Dominicans
vites, Augustinians, Premonstratensians, M
Carmelites, and Benedictines.

14. May a person belong to several Third O

No; persons belonging to one Third Order
not join another without relinquishing their
bership in the former. They are, however, f
affiliate with sodalities or other pious associ
not recognized by the Church as orders.

15. What is the Third Order of St. Francis?

The Third Order of St. Francis is an assoc
of seculars, who wear a distinctive habit, and,
the government of the First or the Third
Regular, live according to a rule of life drawn
St. Francis and approved by the Church.

16. Is the Third Order a true order?

Yes; it is a true order and not a mere pious
ety or confraternity; first, because it has bee
clared to be a true order by the Sovereign Po

and secondly, because the members thereof, devoting their life to the Evangelical Counsels according to an approved rule and under the authority of ecclesiastical superiors, lead a life not unlike that of members of religious orders properly so called.

17. Is then the Third Order Secular a religious order properly so called?

The Third Order Secular lacks the three essential religious vows of poverty, chastity, and obedience and life in the community. Still, it may be styled a religious order in as far as its aim is that of religious orders, and it has much in common with the religious orders properly so called.

18. What is the purpose of the Third Order?

Its purpose was aptly defined by St. Francis when he said to Blessed Lucius, "I have been thinking for some time to establish a third order in which persons living in the world may serve God in a perfect manner."

19. How was the Third Order founded?

It was founded by St. Francis when, in the year 1221, he received as the first Tertiaries the Blessed Lucius and his wife Bonadonna. The Order was soon after approved by the Church, which has not ceased to recommend it to the faithful.

20. Did the Third Order grow and prosper?

Yes; from its very beginning the Third Order enjoyed a rapid and marvelous growth; today it has a membership of quite four millions.

21. Does the Third Order number among its members also illustrious personages?

Yes; popes, bishops, priests, emperors, kings, princes, men of great renown in the world of art and science and literature, in fine, illustrious Christians from all walks of life have deemed it an honor and a privilege to belong to this Order.

22. What influence did the Third Order exert on Society?

The good influence it exerted on Society is inestimable. Through the Third Order great numbers of Christians were gained over to the faithful observance of the Divine commandments, and Society at large profited greatly by the principles of concord, charity, poverty, and humility which the Order tends to promote among its members.

23. Does the Third Order of St. Francis enjoy any spiritual privileges?

Yes; the Church has been pleased to favor the Third Order with many and great spiritual privilges.

24. Is the Third Order suited to all states and conditions of life?

Yes; the Third Order is suited to all Christians, to the most lowly as well as to the most exalted. The great number of sainted men and women from every walk of life whom this Order has produced shows that it offers powerful means of sanctity to all Christians, regardless of their rank or station or occupation.

25. Who are the patrons of the Third Order?

The Church has named St. Louis, King of France, patron of the Brothers; and St. Elizabeth of Thuringia, patron of the Sisters.

26. Is it opportune at the present day to enter the Third Order?

Yes; it is more opportune now than ever to enter the Third Order, in order to revive in oneself and in others the Christian spirit, which is rapidly dying out in many places. This is also the Church's sentiment, repeatedly expressed in these latter days by every Pope, from Leo XIII to our day.

CHAPTER III
Requirements for Admission

27. What is required of those who wish to join the Third Order?

They must be fourteen years of age, of good morals, peace-loving, exact in the practice of the Faith, of tried obedience to the Church. For married women the consent of their husband is likewise required.

28. What is the first requirement for admission?

The first requirement is thus stated in the Rule: "Only those may be received as members who have completed their fourteenth year." In fixing this age, the Church shows how much it desires that even children be interested in an institution whose purpose it is to teach the first steps in religious life.

29. What is the second requirement?

The Rule says they must be "of good character." There is no question here of tried virtue or consummate perfection, but only of good Christian morals, such as are the mark of every practical Catholic.

30. What is the third requirement?

The Rule demands that aspirants be "peace-loving," because without union of hearts and minds no fraternity can prosper or achieve any good.

31. What is the fourth requirement?

The postulant must be "of tried fidelity in the practice of the Catholic Faith"; that is to say, the practice of his faith must be in accord with the doctrine and tradition of the Catholic Church, and must, in consequence, be based on a sufficient knowledge of his religion.

32. What is the fifth requirement?

The postulants must be loyal "to the Roman Church and to the Apostolic See."

33. How must loyalty manifest itself?

It must manifest itself in perfect submission to all dogmatic, moral, and disciplinary decisions of the Church, and in profound respect for the Pope, the bishops, and the priests, especially the parish priests.

34. What does the Rule say regarding the admission of married women?

The Rule says, married women are not to be admitted without the knowledge and consent of their husband; if it is thought necessary to act otherwise, it should be done only on the motion of the priest who is the judge of their conscience.

35. What is to be said of this injunction?

It is admirably designed to preserve the peace of families without, however, imposing on women any restraint prejudicial to their spiritual welfare; for, the Rule expressly states that this condition may be dispensed with whenever the confessor of the woman deems it advisable.

CHAPTER IV

Reception of Novices

36. Is it necessary to have a religious vocation in order to enter the Third Order?

No; it is not necessary to have a religious vocation in order to become a member of the Third Order; it is sufficient to have the qualities demanded by the Rule and a desire for Christian perfection.

37. To become a Tertiary, is it necessary to join a fraternity of the Third Order?

No; if necessity demands, one may be admitted as an isolated Tertiary. After being received, however, such a Tertiary must make a year's novitiate, and then pronounce his profession as soon as possible.

38. How must an isolated Tertiary conduct himself?

A Tertiary who for some grave reason cannot enter a fraternity of the Third Order, must strive conscientiously to learn and to fulfill the precepts of the Rule, and, as much as possible, to keep in touch with the Order; for, to be an isolated Tertiary does not mean to be a negligent and an independent member.

39. Is it advantageous to belong to a fraternity of the Third Order?

Yes; it is of great advantage to belong to a regular fraternity, both on account of the spiritual instruction and advancement, on account of the privileges and indulgences to be gained by the members attending the monthly meetings, and because fraternal life is a characteristic of the Order.

40. What must one do to become a member of the Third Order?

A person desiring to become a member, must make application to the local Director of the Third Order or to his representative, and, if it is agreeable, the applicant at once enters upon the postulate, which lasts till the day fixed by the Director for the reception or investment.

41. How does the reception take place?

The reception into the Third Order takes place in the following manner: On the appointed day, the postulant presents himself to a priest having the necessary faculties and says: "Reverend Father, I humbly ask of you the habit of the Third Order of Penance, in order that with it I may more easily obtain eternal salvation." Thereupon, the postulant receives from the priest the habit, the cord, and the lighted candle.

42. What does the habit signify?

The habit of penance with which the Tertiary is clothed, signifies that he must divest himself of the old man with his acts and clothe himself with the new man "who is created according to God in justice and holiness of truth."

43. What does the cord symbolize?

The cord symbolizes holy purity, which the Tertiary must preserve by controlling in himself the passion of lust, "that the virtue of continency and chastity may dwell in him."

44. What does the lighted candle signify?

It signifies the light of Christ, communicated to the Tertiary by the Seraphic form of life, "that being dead to the world, he may live for God shunning the works of darkness."

45. What does the Rule prescribe regarding the habit?

The Rule says, "The members shall wear the small scapular and the cord as prescribed; if they do not, they deprive themselves of the rights and privileges of the Order."

46. What is to be noted regarding this precept?

It is to be noted, first, that the Tertiary must never be without his scapular and cord; and, secondly, that he who, without sufficient reason, fails to wear them, deprives himself of the privileges of the Order.

47. What is to be said regarding the wearing of the large habit of the Third Order?

The large habit or tunic of brown wool may be outwardly worn only at the monthly reunions of the members and at certain ecclesiastical functions; namely, processions, pilgrimages, general communions, and funerals, provided the members attend in a body. Tertiaries may be likewise clothed in the large habit at the time of their death and burial.

48. What does the Rule say regarding the novitiate?

The Rule simply says that all who enter the Third Order, whether men or women, shall make a year's novitiate. In order that the profession may be valid, it may not be made before the day following the anniversary of the reception of the habit; on the other hand, the term of the novitiate should not be prolonged indefinitely.

49. Do the novices enjoy any privileges of the Order?

Yes; the novices participate in the spiritual privileges of the Order, provided they fulfill the obligations, especially that of wearing the habit.

50. What should a novice do when he is tempted to leave the Order?

He should ask of God the grace of perseverance, and, if necessary, he should disclose the temptation to the Director.

51. Should a novice ardently desire the grace of profession?

Yes; the novice should have an ardent desire to give himself to God by making profession in the Third Order; accordingly, he should endeavor to render himself worthy of this grace by devout prayer and earnest preparation and by fidelity in observing the Rule.

CHAPTER V

Profession of Members

52. What does the Rule say regarding the profession of members?

The Rule says that, after a full year's novitiate, the novices shall duly make their profession of the Rule of the Order, shall promise to observe the laws of God, to obey the Church, and, if they fail in their profession, to make the required satisfaction.

53. How is the profession made?

According to the ceremonial, the novice clothed in the large habit of the Order, or at least wearing outwardly the scapular and the cord, kneels before the altar, at the feet of the priest, and with hands joined pronounces the formula of profession.

54. How does this formula read?

This formula reads as follows: "I, — —, in the presence of Almighty God, in honor of the Immaculate Virgin Mary, of Blessed Father Francis, and of all the Saints, promise to observe all the time of my life the commandments of God and the Rule of the Third Order, instituted by the same Blessed Francis, according to the form approved by Nicholas IV and Leo XIII; also to satisfy at the pleasure of the Visitor for transgressions committed against the same Rule."

55. Is the profession made in the Third Order a sacred act?

Yes; it is sacred in itself and in its effects. For this reason, it is attended with holy ceremonies and made in the presence of Almighty God, in honor of the Immaculate Virgin Mary, of Blessed Father Francis, and of all the Saints.

56. What is the nature of this profession?

The profession in the Third Order is of its nature not a vow, but a pledge of one's word, which should be respected in virtue of the acceptance of the Church and of the fidelity one owes to one's given word.

57. For how long a time does the Tertiary bind himself?

He binds himself for life; for he says, "I promise to observe the Rule of the Third Order all the time of my life."

58. Is anyone ever permitted to leave the Third Order?

One may leave the Third Order to enter a religious order or congregation. A person who leaves the Third Order for any reason, does not commit a sin, but he deprives himself of many graces and means of sanctification.

59. Which are the means of persevering in the Order?

These means are: A thorough knowledge of the Rule and the benefits of the Order; a great devotion to St. Francis; an ardent desire for perfection, and an exact observance of the precepts of the Rule.

60. What is the first thing Tertiaries promise in their profession?

They pledge themselves to observe the laws of God and of the Church. By making this promise they bind themselves more closely to the service of God, but contract no new obligation.

61. What is the second thing Tertiaries promise?

They promise to observe "the Rule of the Third Order, instituted by the Blessed Father Francis." This Rule, however, is not strictly preceptive, but merely directive, hence not binding under sin.

62. What is the third thing Tertiaries promise?

They promise "to satisfy at the pleasure of the Visitor for transgressions committed against the Rule."

63. What is the reward promised to the faithful Tertiaries?

The priest, having accepted the profession of the Tertiary, replies: "And I, on the part of God, if thou observest these things, promise thee life everlasting." In these words is contained a great consolation for every true child of St. Francis.

64. May a Tertiary pass from one fraternity of the Order to another?

Yes; he may do so with the consent of the respective superiors. In this connection, it is to be noted that a Tertiary may gain the indulgences, and receive the General Absolution even in a fraternity other than his own.

65. Which is the greatest benefit that Tertiaries derive from their profession?

The greatest benefit that Tertiaries derive from their profession, consists in this that their whole life is regulated by a Rule approved by the Church and capable of leading them to a high degree of sanctity. In fact, the Rule of the Third Order is nothing but the law of the Gospel applied to the condition of people living in the world.

66. Should Tertiaries faithfully observe the Rule?

Yes; even if the Rule does not oblige under pain of sin, they should, nevertheless, observe it in order to be true to their promise, and to participate in the benefits of the Franciscan form of life.

CHAPTER VI

Practice of Penance

67. What does the Rule prescribe as to the exterior life of Tertiaries?

The Rule says, "In all things let the members of the Third Order avoid extremes of cost and style, observing the golden mean suited to each one's station in life."

68. What does this precept imply?

It implies the avoidance of luxury and vain display, and moderation in all things.

69. What is luxury?

Luxury is the free indulgence in costly foods, dress, furniture, or anything expensive which merely gratifies the appetites or tastes.

70. Is luxury pernicious?

Yes; it is pernicious from the Christian and moral standpoint, because it fosters selfishness and, in general, is the source of many spiritual evils.

71. What kind of display of dress and ornament is forbidden by the Rule?

The Rule forbids all vain and excessive display, inasmuch as it is an obstacle to sanctification and edification.

72. Is a Tertiary permitted to conform in all things to the fashions of the day?

No; for by so doing he would very often act contrary to his vocation not only as Tertiary, but even as Christian.

73. What is prescribed on the subject of luxury and display?

It is prescribed that Tertiaries observe the rules of moderation in so far as they apply to each one's state of life. Hence, they may use the goods of this world according to their state or rank, but they should take care to avoid all extravagance and worldliness.

74. What does the Rule say on the subject of amusements?

The Rule says, "Let them with the utmost caution keep away from dances and shows which savor of license, as well as from all forms of dissipation."

75. Are Tertiaries never permitted to attend a dance?

As a general rule the Brothers and Sisters of Penance should avoid dancing and dances, even when they are otherwise unobjectionable, though in the latter case it would not be forbidden to attend, particularly with the consent of the Father Director.

76. How should a Tertiary, who is forced to attend a dance or ball, conduct himself?

If, by way of exception, a Tertiary attends a dance or ball, he must conduct himself according to the rules of prudence and modesty, and by his interior dispositions render remote the dangers of sin.

77. What does the rule say of shows?

Tertiaries should refrain with the utmost caution from objectionable shows if they do not wish to suffer the loss of their faith and good morals, or, at least, of the Franciscan spirit.

78. Are Tertiaries never allowed to assist at dramatic presentations?

Yes; Tertiaries may assist at them as long as they are reasonably certain that nothing objectionable will be presented.

79. What is prescribed regarding repasts?

The Rule prescribes frugality in eating and drinking. This implies that Tertiaries should not only not eat and drink to excess, but also cultivate habits of restraint by not eating and drinking for the mere pleasure of it.

80. How should their repasts be sanctified?

The Rule says, "(Let them) devoutly say grace before and after meals." This Christian practice should be fostered above all by Tertiaries.

81. What is prescribed by the Rule as to fasting and abstinence?

"They shall fast on the Vigil of the Immaculate Conception and on that of St. Francis; they are to be highly commended who, according to the original Rule of the Tertiaries, also either fast on Fridays or abstain from fleshmeat on Wednesdays."

82. How should Tertiaries observe the law of fasting and abstinence?

They should observe with courage and fidelity the fasts and abstinences prescribed by the Church and not ask for a dispensation from them unless forced by necessity; and if their condition permits, they should abstain on Wednesdays or fast on Fridays, as counseled by the Rule.

CHAPTER VII

Holy Sacraments — Divine Office — Last Will

83. What does the Rule prescribe on the subject of Confession?

The Rule says, "They shall approach the Sacrament of Penance every month." They are, therefore, commanded to confess at least once a month, because the Sacrament of Penance is a powerful means of preserving and increasing sanctifying grace and leading a virtuous life.

84. With what disposition should Tertiaries confess their sins?

They should make each confession as if it were their last one. Hence, they should carefully examine their conscience, make a good act of contrition and a sincere confession, and receive the imparted absolution with the same reverence as if it were the most precious blood of our Savior poured over their souls in remission of their sins.

85. What does the Rule say regarding Holy Communion?

The Rule says, "They shall approach the Sacrament of the Holy Eucharist every month." In prescribing monthly Communion, the Rule indicates the least that is expected of Tertiaries. True children of Mother Church and of St. Francis, however, will receive oftener.

86. How often should Tertiaries approach the Holy Table?

If possible, every day; for, this is the express wish of Holy Mother Church and the ardent desire of her Divine Founder.

87. Why should Tertiaries receive so often?

For the good of their souls and the edification of their neighbor.

88. How should they receive Holy Communion?

They should receive Holy Communion in the state of grace, with the right intention, and with all the fervor of which they are capable.

89. Should Tertiaries abstain from Holy Communion if they feel little or no devotion?

No; for true devotion consists not in pious feelings, but in the determined will to honor God by acts of piety.

90. Which is the daily prayer prescribed for Tertiaries?

The daily prayer prescribed for Tertiaries is the Divine Office.

91. What is the Divine Office?

It is a formula of prayers daily recited by the members of the clergy and of the religious orders, according to the form laid down by the Church.

92. Why is this office prescribed for the members of the Third Order?

Because the members of the Third Order are to be regarded as religious living in the world, and as such they have the obligation as well as the privilege of sharing in the worship of praise daily offered to God by religious properly so called.

93. What does the Rule say regarding the Divine Office?

"Tertiaries among the clergy, since they recite the Divine Office daily, shall be under no further obligation in this regard. Lay members who recite neither the Canonical Hours, nor the Little Office of the Blessed Virgin Mary, shall say daily twelve Our Fathers, Hail Marys and Glorys, unless they are prevented by ill health."

94. Does the Rule impose on clerical Tertiaries any special obligation regarding the Divine Office?

No; the Rule does not impose on them any special obligation in this respect since they are already obligated to say the Divine Office by the law of the Church.

95. What form of prayer is prescribed for lay Tertiaries?

Lay Tertiaries are obliged to recite either the Little Office of the Blessed Virgin or the office of the twelve Our Fathers, Hail Marys, and Glorys.

96. At what time of the day should lay Tertiaries say their office?

They may say their office at any time convenient to them.

97. May Tertiaries be dispensed from reciting their office?

Yes; they may be dispensed, but only for the reason of ill health.

98. What should those Tertiaries do who cannot find time to recite their daily office?

A good Tertiary will always find time to say his office. In case, however, it should be impossible for him to say the entire office, he will say at least a part of it, or perform some other good work instead.

99. Does any special merit or efficacy attach to the Divine Office?

Yes; the Divine Office is more meritorious and more efficacious than any private prayer, because it is the prayer of the Church, the beloved Spouse of Christ.

100. What is prescribed regarding the making of one's last will?

The Rule says, "Let those who are entitled to make a will, do so in good time."

101. What does this precept imply?

It does not imply that Tertiaries must deprive themselves of the ownership or the enjoyment of their earthly goods, but only that they make their will in good time.

102. Why does the Rule impose this obligation on Tertiaries?

The Rule imposes this obligation on Tertiaries in order that they may practice the virtue of detachment and the spirit of poverty, and may forestall any quarrel such as generally arises in a family or a society at the death of an intestate person.

103. Why should Tertiaries faithfully observe this injunction?

They should faithfully observe this injunction in order to provide for the peace of their own soul and the peace of their family.

CHAPTER VIII
Good Example — Exercises of Piety

104. What does the Rule say on the subject of good example?

The Rule says that in their daily life Tertiaries should study to lead others by their example.

105. Wherein does a good example consist?

It consists in fulfilling, always and everywhere, whether in public or in private, one's duties, particularly those of one's state of life.

106. Which is the first duty of one's state?

It is the duty of fulfilling, in a Christian manner, one's obligations toward the various members of one's family. This is a duty of primary importance, and he who is negligent in this, cannot be a worthy member of the Third Order.

107. How should this duty be performed?

It should be performed in accordance with the will of God. Husbands and wives should, therefore, preserve inviolate their mutual marriage promise; parents should bring up their children in the fear of God; and children, on their part, should revere, love and obey their parents.

108. How should mothers and mistresses of the household set a good example?

They should set a good example by governing their subjects according to the principles of justice, charity, and patience, and by regulating the affairs of the household according to the laws of order and economy.

109. How should a Tertiary engaged in business conduct himself?

He should endeavor to edify his customers by his willingness to serve them and by conducting his business along the lines of honesty.

110. How should a Tertiary laborer give a good example?

He should give a good example by conscientiously performing the work assigned to him, without, however, neglecting the service of God and the care of his soul.

111. How may Tertiaries edify their fellow parishioners?

Tertiaries may edify the other members of the parish by assisting regularly at Holy Mass and at the other exercises of devotion, and by taking an active part in everything that concerns the welfare of the parish.

112. What should be the attitude of Tertiaries in parochial affairs?

In accordance with their vocation, their attitude should be one of humility and self-sacrifice. It should, therefore, be their ambition not to rule the affairs of the parish, but to serve in executing the commands of their ecclesiastical superiors.

113. How should Tertiaries conduct themselves toward their priests?

Being disciples of Saint Francis, who during his lifetime had the highest regard for priests, Tertiaries should at all times and under all circumstances show respect and obedience to the ministers of God.

114. What does the Rule say regarding exercises of piety?

The Rule says, "Let them strive to promote practices of piety and good works."

115. Does the Rule specify these pious practices?

No; the Rule does not specify what pious practices should be promoted; it contents itself with recommending the approved practices of piety in general.

116. How should a Tertiary perform his exercises of piety?

Having prudently chosen such exercises as are best suited to his vocation and to his needs, the Tertiary should strive to perform them faithfully and devoutly.

117. What place should these exercises occupy in the Tertiary's spiritual life?

These exercises should never become a hindrance in fulfilling one's other duties: hence, while striving to remain faithful to his pious practices, the Tertiary should, nevertheless, maintain a certain freedom in performing them.

CHAPTER IX

Bad Literature — Fraternal Charity

118. What does the Rule enjoin on Tertiaries in regard to bad literature?

The Rule says, "Let them not allow books or publications which are a menace to virtue, to be brought into their homes, or to be read by those under their care." This precept is based on the natural law, which forbids us to expose ourselves to voluntary occasions of sin and to co-operate in the evil actions of others.

119. What does this passage of the Rule imply?

It implies a twofold negative precept; namely, not to allow bad literature to be brought into one's house, and not to allow those over whom one is placed to read bad books or papers.

120. What is, therefore, the duty of parents and masters?

It is their duty to keep careful watch over the reading of their charges and to forbid them all books or papers that might be injurious to their faith or virtue.

121. Is there any excuse for reading bad books or papers?

No; for the common Christian there is none whatever, and one cannot sufficiently deplore the blindness of so many who, in spite of admonitions to the contrary, wilfully poison their minds by reading irreligious or immoral books and papers.

122. What does the Rule prescribe regarding the mutual relation of Tertiaries?

The Rule prescribes, "Let them earnestly maintain the spirit of charity among themselves and toward others." These words call to the minds of Tertiaries the favorite commandment of our Divine Savior and the touching admonitions of his faithful servant St. Francis regarding fraternal charity.

123. What is the extent of this charity?

This charity should embrace all men without exception; hence, not only the members of one's family or fraternity, but also strangers and enemies.

124. What is the chief characteristic of the charity of Tertiaries?

According to the Rule, it is kindness or benevolence, which consists in wishing well to others from all our heart.

125. How should this benevolence show itself?

It should show itself not only in words, but also in deeds, for charitable deeds are the best proof of a benevolent disposition.

126. Which are the commonest faults against charity?

The commonest faults against charity are those of the tongue; against these, therefore, Tertiaries should be particularly on their guard if they would not destroy charity in themselves and in others.

127. What does the Rule say regarding violations of charity?

It says that Tertiaries should take care to settle quarrels whenever they can do so. Hence, it is their special duty to act as peacemakers.

128. How should Tertiaries fulfill this duty?

Tertiaries should endeavor to heal discord by reconciling those at odds. In this matter, however, they should be guided by the rules of prudence, and if they are wanting in the necessary tact, they should refer the question at issue to their superiors, or recommend the affair to God in devout prayer.

129. What is the scope of this precept?

According to their Rule, Tertiaries are required to settle quarrels whenever they can do so; that is to say, within and without the Order, in private and in public life.

130. What obligation does the Rule impose on Tertiaries in regard to oaths?

The Rule prescribes that they never take an oath except in case of necessity. This precept implies nothing but what is already contained in the second commandment of God.

CHAPTER X

Special Exercises of Piety— Mutual Aid

131. What does the Rule prescribe in regard to the examination of one's conscience?

The Rule prescribes that Tertiaries should examine their conscience every night.

132. Why was this precept given particularly to Tertiaries?

Because Tertiaries should be persons, not merely of ordinary religious fidelity, but of deep and consistent piety, and there is no spiritual exercise so conducive to piety and religiousness as the daily examen of conscience.

133. In what way does this practice aid Tertiaries in acquiring perfection?

It aids them in acquiring perfection by revealing to them not only their daily transgressions, but also their predominant passions, which are responsible for most of their sins, and which constitute the chief drawback to their spiritual progress.

134. How should Tertiaries make their daily exa-

men that it may be conducive to their spiritual progress?

They should make it not in a slipshod and hasty way, but with method and earnestness.

135. On what points should they examine themselves?

They should examine themselves on the commandments of God and on the precepts of the Rule.

136. What does the Rule inculcate on Tertiaries in regard to hearing Mass?

The Rule says, "Let those who can do so, attend Mass daily"; hence, those whose circumstances allow, should make a practice of assisting at Mass every day, or at least as often as they can do so without great trouble, in order to become partakers of the inestimable spirtual blessings of which this august Sacrifice is the source and center.

137. How may Tertiaries who cannot assist at Mass daily, comply with the spirit of this injunction?

They may do so by attending Mass on Sundays with punctuality and reverence, and by trying to induce as many negligent Catholics as possible to do likewise.

138. What method should Tertiaries follow in hearing Mass?

A good and easy way to hear Mass devoutly, is to follow the prayer book or to recite the Rosary of the Sorrowful Mysteries. A devout method is that of St. Leonard of Port Maurice, which is found in almost all Third Order manuals. Those who can do so without too much distraction, may use the Missal.

139. What does the Rule say regarding monthly meetings of the fraternity?

The Rule says briefly, "Let them attend the monthly meetings called by the Prefect." Attendance at these meetings is necessary to foster and maintain in the members the Tertiary spirit.

140. Should Tertiaries easily dispense themselves from such attendance?

Tertiaries who have at heart the interest of their Order, will not easily dispense themselves from attending the monthly meeting, lest, by their example, they induce others to do the same, and thus bring on the ruin of their fraternity.

141. What does the Rule enjoin on Tertiaries in the matter of contributions?

"Let them contribute according to their means to a common fund, from which the poorer members may be aided, especially in time of sickness, or provision may be made for the dignity of Divine Worship."

142. How should Tertiaries fulfill this injunction of the Rule?

They should do so generously and discreetly; that is, each member should contribute according to his means, and no one should contribute above his means.

143. Why should Tertiaries be particularly faithful in complying with this precept?

Because care for the poor and concern for the dignity of Divine worship were two of the characteristic traits of St. Francis; hence, they should be likewise the distinguishing features of all who aspire to the perfection of his Rule.

144. What special duties does the Rule impose on the Officers in regard to sick members?

The Rule says, "Let the officers either personally visit a sick member, or send some one to perform the services of charity."

145. What does this precept imply?

It implies that the duty of visiting the sick is especially incumbent on the Prefect of each fraternity; when he, however, is unable for any reason to make these visits of charity, he may delegate some one else to call in his stead.

146. What are the Officers commanded to do in a case of serious illness of a member?

They are commanded to "remind and urge the sick person to arrange in time the affairs of his soul."

147. What are Tertiaries to observe in regard to the funeral of a deceased member?

"At the funeral of a deceased member the resident

and visiting Tertiaries shall assemble and sa
common five decades of the Rosary for the soι
the departed."

**148. What else does the Rule prescribe for the r
of deceased members?**

The Rule prescribes that "the priests at the I
Sacrifice and the lay members, if possible, ha
received Holy Communion, pray with fervent c
ity for the eternal rest of the deceased."

CHAPTER XI

Organization and Government of the Third Order

149. What is meant by a fraternity of the Third Order?

A fraternity is an association of Tertiaries canonically established, with the permission of the bishop, by the religious superiors of the Franciscan Order or by priests specially delegated for this purpose.

150. What persons are capable of forming a fraternity?

The persons capable of forming a fraternity are the professed members of the Third Order Secular, united in a sufficient number to insure the progress of the Tertiary congregation.

151. How should the Tertiaries be disposed toward their fraternity?

The Tertiaries should love their fraternity, and should interest themselves in everything that pertains to its welfare, either by laboring to recruit and to organize it, or by devoting themselves to the good works prescribed or advocated by it.

152. What is prescribed in regard to the offices of a fraternity?

•The Rule says, "The offices shall be conferred at a meeting of the members."

153. How are these offices assigned?

The first officers are appointed by the Visitor or Director when the fraternity is established; thereafter they are elected by the professed members of the congregation at regular intervals.

154. How long do the officials remain in office?

The Rule says, "The term of these offices shall be three years."

155. Are the members free to decline an office?

On this point, the Rule declares that no one can, without good reason, refuse any office tendered him.

156· How should the office-holders discharge their duties?

The Rule says in a general way, "no one is to discharge the duties of his office negligently."·

157. What should the officers bear in mind?

They should bear in mind that upon their zeal, prudence, docility, and tact depend the usefulness and efficiency, if not the very life and existence, of the fraternity.

158. By what name are the superiors of the Third Order collectively designated?

The board of officers is called the Fraternity Council.

49

159. Who is the chief official with regard to a fraternity?

It is the Reverend Director, representing the superiors of the First or the Third Order Regular, who are the canonical authorities of the Third Order.

160. Which is the chief office in the fraternity itself?

The chief office in the fraternity itself is that of the Prefect.

161. Which is the principal office after that of Prefect?

It is that of Assistant or Vice Prefect; like the Prefect, he is to preside at the meetings and to conduct the business of the fraternity in the absence of the Director and of the Prefect.

162. Is there any other important charge besides those mentioned?

Yes; it is that of Master and Mistress of Novices, who are appointed in the larger fraternities to assist the superiors in instructing the novices.

163. Which are the other offices usually assigned in a fraternity?

They are those of Secretary, Treasurer, Sacristan, Infirmarian or Nurse, and Promoters.

164. What is the means of preserving the discipline of the Third Order?

This means is the canonical visit, concerning which the Rule says: "The Visitor, who is charged with the supervision of the Order, shall diligently investigate whether the Rule is properly observed. Therefore, it shall be his duty to visit the Fraternities every year, or oftener if need be, and hold a meeting, to which all the officers and members shall be summoned."

165. Which are the powers of the Visitor and the duties of the Tertiaries toward him?

These powers and duties are clearly indicated in the Rule, which ordains: "Should the Visitor recall a member to his duty by admonition or command, or impose a salutary penance, let such member meekly accept the correction and not refuse to perform the penance."

166. Who are to be appointed to the office of Visitor?

"The Visitors are to be chosen from the First Franciscan Order, or from the Third Order Regular and shall be appointed by the provincial or local superiors when requested. Laymen cannot hold the office of Visitor."

167. What does the Rule ordain in regard to disobedient members?

"Disobedient and harmful members shall be admonished of their duty a second and a third time; if they do not submit, let them be dismissed from the Order."

168. How does the Rule oblige the members?

"Those who offend against any provision of this Rule, do not incur the guilt of sin unless in so doing they also transgress the Commandments of God or of the Church."

169. May a person be dispensed from any provision of the Rule?

"Should a just and serious cause prevent a member from observing any provision of the Rule, such person may be dispensed therefrom, or the regulation may be prudently commuted."

170. Who has power to dispense from the Rule?

The faculty or power of granting such dispensation or commutation rests with the superiors of the Franciscan Order. By special delegation, other priests may likewise dispense from the Rule.

CHAPTER XII

Indulgences — Privileges — Spirit of the Third Order

171. What is an indulgence?

An indulgence is the remission of the temporal punishment due to sin after the sin has been forgiven, by applying to a person the superabundant merits and satisfactions of our Savior, of the Blessed Virgin Mary, and of the Saints.

172. How many kinds of indulgences are there?

There are two kinds; namely, plenary and partial indulgences.

173. Which are the conditions usually required to gain a plenary indulgence?

The conditions commonly required are: Confession, communion, and prayer for the intention of the Holy Father.

174. Is there any time or place specified for gaining indulgences?

There are indulgences for the gaining of which the Church has specified neither time nor place; a great number of them, however, may be gained only on certain days and in certain places.

175. Is the Third Order rich in indulgences?

Yes; it is very rich in indulgences, plenary and partial; and these spiritual favors, apart from the many other graces and advantages enjoyed by the Tertiaries, ought to be a powerful inducement to enter the Order.

176. What is the Papal Blessing?

It is a solemn invocation by which the Holy Father the Pope calls down the Divine assistance on the faithful, and with which there is connected a plenary indulgence.

177. Does the Holy Father sometimes delegate others to bestow this blessing?

Yes; the Holy Father frequently empowers bishops and priests to bestow this blessing in his name. The Directors of the Third Order enjoy this privilege in virtue of their Office. The Tertiaries assembled in a body may receive it twice a year.

178. What is the General Absolution?

The General Absolution or Indulgenced Blessing is a solemn invocation which partakes of the nature of a sacramental, and to which there is attached a plenary indulgence.

179. What are the conditions for gaining the ple-

nary indulgence attached to this General Absolution or Indulgenced Blessing?

The conditions are, reception of the Sacraments of Penance and of the Holy Eucharist, and prayers for the intention of the Pope. A special visit to a church is not required.

180. By whom may this absolution or blessing be imparted?

It may be imparted either privately by the Father Confessor in the confessional, or publicly in a meeting of Tertiaries by the Reverend Director or, in his absence, by any priest who has the faculties of the diocese.

181. When may Tertiaries receive the Indulgenced Blessing in the confessional?

Tertiaries may receive the Indulgenced Blessing in the confessional on the day preceding the feast for which it is granted, or on the feast itself, or on any day during the week following.

182. When may sick and convalescent Tertiaries receive the Indulgenced Blessing?

Sick and convalescent Tertiaries may receive it on any day within the week following the day for which it is granted.

183. What is the Franciscan Crown?

It is the rosary of the seven joys of the Blessed Virgin Mary taught by her to a Franciscan friar in 1422. It is enriched with many indulgences.

184. Are Tertiaries required to have beads specially blessed to gain the plenary indulgence granted them by Pope Leo XIII for the recitation of the Crown?

No; Tertiaries may gain this indulgence without beads especially blessed, or, for that matter, without any beads whatever, and that as often as they recite the Crown. But they must have a blessed crown to gain certain indulgences granted to the Crown by Pope Pius X.

185. Is it necessary to meditate on the mysteries while reciting this rosary?

No; meditation on the mysteries is not required; it is sufficient to recite the Paters and Aves prescribed.

186. What indulgences can the faithful in general gain by the recitation of the Crown?

They may gain a plenary indulgence if they recite the Crown together with the Tertiaries. When they recite it privately, they must have beads especially blessed for the purpose; and they can then gain also the numerous plenary and partial indulgences granted by Pope Pius X.

187. What is meant by the Franciscan spirit?

Like every other religious institution, the Third Order also has its proper spirit, which is no other than the spirit of the Seraphic Founder, whose aim it was to imitate as closely as possible our Savior Jesus Christ.

Prayer of a Tertiary
to St. Francis

O Seraphic St. Francis, my beloved Father, protector of the poor, glorious founder of the three great Orders, with tender love and veneration I kneel before thee and kiss the sacred stigmata with which our Divine Savior adorned thee. I thank thee for having numbered me among thy children. This grace is so sublime, that I could never have merited it for myself; and it brings with it an endless chain of Heaven's choicest blessings. How shall I ever be able to show thee sufficient gratitude for all these favors?

O Holy Father, help me ever to love the Third Order most tenderly. Let me regard it as my spiritual home and my paradise on earth, that I may, ever mindful of my holy profession, keep the commandments of God and of the Church, and observe most faithfully even the smallest details of the Rule. For only then shall I receive the wholesome effects of the blessing which thou, in thy dying hour, didst impart to thy beloved children. Bless me, therefore, kind Father, bless thy unworthy child, that I may persevere in the conscientious observance of the Rule of the Third Order until the end of my life. Amen.

The Third Order Secular of St. Francis

Origin and Organization

THE Third Order Secular of St. Francis must be regarded as a natural and necessary product of the Franciscan movement which began with the spread of the Order of Friars Minor and throughout the subsequent centuries exerted so wide and beneficent an influence on Society. So profound was the impression which the preaching and example of St. Francis and his first disciples made on the people that thousands from every age and walk flocked to them and asked to join their ranks. In many cases family ties stood in the way, so that large numbers had to be dismissed. Evidently, this rising flood of religious enthusiasm had to be checked or led into proper channels. "It was on this account," writes Pope Leo XIII, in his famous encyclical **Auspicato** of September 17, 1882, "that the most holy man determined to institute the Brotherhood of the Third Order, which was to admit all ranks, all ages, both sexes, and yet in no way necessitate the rupture of family or social ties."

The Rule of the Third Order consisted only in obedience to God and to his Church, in avoiding factions and quarrels, and in no way defrauding one's neighbor. The members were to take up arms only for the defense of religion and country; to be moderate in food and in clothing; to shun luxury; and to abstain from the dangerous seduction of dances and plays. Such was the simple rule of life which St. Francis, counseled by his friend Cardinal Ugolino, drew up for his Third Order, and according to which persons living in the world were to put into practice his ideals of Christian perfection.

According to the better opinion, based on the authority of Mariano of Florence and on the earliest Papal bull known to exist on the subject, the Third Order was organized near Florence, Italy. As the date of its organization the best historians justly assign the year 1221, basing their opinion on the fact that the oldest preserved rule of the Third Order, discovered by Sabatier, bears this date. That same year, 1221, St. Francis came to Poggibonzi, a town near Florence. Here he met one Lucius, or Lucchese, a friend of his boyhood days and now a prosperous merchant. He was a man of singular virtue, and, having heard how the saint had founded an order for seculars at Florence, he asked to be enrolled. St. Francis gladly complied, and vested him and his wife, Bonadonna, with the habit of the Third Order. These two, therefore, are commonly regarded as the first Tertiaries. About the same time, a certain lawyer of the Roman Curia, by the name of Bartholomew, was clothed with the Tertiary habit and granted faculties to vest others, thereby becoming the first Third Order director.

During the thirteenth century the members of the Third Order, which had meanwhile spread to every part of Europe, followed different rules and stood more or less under episcopal jurisdiction. In 1289, however, Pope Nicholas IV, wishing to unite these scattered fraternities so as to make them a more powerful force in the Church, gave them a uniform and definite rule and placed them once and for all under the jurisdiction of the Order of Friars Minor.

It was in 1883 that Pope Leo XIII, himself a fervent Tertiary, breathed new life and vigor into the Third Order by publishing his constitution, Misericors Dei Filius. The illustrious pontiff knew what the order had meant for the moral and religious life of the masses in the Ages of Faith, and realized how, in consequence of the Protestant Reformation with its two centuries of wars and revolutions, the nineteenth century was gradually drifting into indifferentism and infidelity. To bring back the nations to God was his one endeavor; and the best means to accomplish this was, in his mind, the Third Order of St. Francis. Accordingly, he issued the famous constitution, in which he revised and modified the rule of the Third Order with a special view to the conditions and needs of modern times. At the same time he granted new and richer favors, indulgences, and privileges to those who would join the Third Order.

In our day much has been done to spread and intrench the blessings of Third Order spirit and life by means of organization. Not only is the fraternal life of the Tertiaries insisted upon locally, but the local fraternities themselves are organized in provinces, and even nationally, with provincial and national boards of officers and with approved provincial and national constitutions, directed toward unifying and stimulating local efforts and giving them permanence.

As a means to keep alive this union of forces, periodical rallies are held among the fraternities of a locality or region, or again the fraternities of a province or a nation gather for a provincial or a national congress.

Every Tertiary and every Fraternity that values the spirit and the aims of the Order, welcomes such organization and supports and cooperates with it to the best of his ability. The Hierarchy of our country itself dignifies the National Tertiary Organization by appointing one of the Hierarchy as Bishop Protector of the Third Order, to link the National Organization of the Order with the body of Bishops, in the National Catholic Welfare Conference. Locally and nationally the Third Order is thus put at the command of the Clergy and the Hierarchy as a mighty auxiliary arm of Catholic Action.

To be sure, after all the Order will never be greater than the goodwill on the part of its membership. It is for this reason that every Tertiary and every Fraternity must seek to grow in appreciation of the aims and destiny of the Order. Intelligent study of the vast and growing literature of the Order, especially of the Papal documents concerning the Order, is therefore imperative wherever there are Tertiaries.

We recommend among other publications above all the organ of the National Tertiary Organization: FRANCISCAN HERALD and FORUM, published at 5045 Laflin Street, Chicago, Illinois. Subscription price for twelve months of the year, $1.00.

THIRD ORDER REQUISITES

THIRD ORDER SCAPULAR AND CORD
Per set **$0.25**

The scapulars measure 2⅜ x 1⅝ inches, silk stitched around the edges, and held together with a thin white silk braid. The cord is of soft material.

THIRD ORDER SHROUDS. **$12.00**
CORD for Shroud. **1.00**
 (When ordering, please state whether for man or woman.)

THE FRANCISCAN CROWN

or the Rosary of the Seven Joys of the Bl. Virgin; the most richly indulgenced Rosary. A Leaflet explaining method of recitation and indulgences sent with each Crown.

 To be had in several styles and at varying prices.

Third Order Fraternity Book. **$0.10**

Contains congregational arrangement of prayers for the meetings.

CARDS with prayers and hymns used at
 meetings . . . . .each **$0.02½**
 per 100 **2.00**

POSTAGE EXTRA

FRANCISCAN HERALD PRESS
1434 West 51st Street
CHICAGO, ILLINOIS

THIRD ORDER REQUISITES
The Tertiaries' Companion

Cloth, red edges. **$0.60**

Contains in compact form matter pertaining to the Third Order: the text of the Rule; the latest indulgences; the Franciscan calendar; the ritual prayers before and after meetings; the ceremonial for the various functions of the Order in both English and Latin texts. The dependable up-to-date manual for Tertiaries, re-edited periodically to conform to the latest decrees.

FRANCISCAN ART CALENDAR

New Edition available every year. A series of beautiful art pictures. Besides containing all essential information wanted and needed in the Catholic home, it serves as a ready reference for Tertiaries on many questions.

Single copies, each. **$0.30**
4 for **1.00**
12 for . . . . **3.00** etc.

To be had at fraternity headquarters or

from

FRANCISCAN HERALD PRESS
1434 West 51st Street
CHICAGO, ILLINOIS

POSTAGE EXTRA

READINGS FOR TERTIARIES

The Better Life—Fr. Kilian, O.F.M. Cap $2.5
   Detailed explanation of the Rule of the Third Order
Heart O' the Rule—Fr. Marion, O.F.M. 1
Piety in Overalls (Matt Talbott)—Robt. J. Bayer 0
White Violet (Margaret Sinclair)—Robt. J. Bayer 0
Take and Read—Fr. Faustin, O.F.M. 0
Paschal Baylon—Louise Malloy 1
Two Sainted Laymen—Fr. Hilarion, O.F.M. 1
Frederick Ozanam—Fr. Faustin, O.F.M. 1
Two Literary Women (Fullerton-Lea) 1
Little Day Book for Tertiaries—Marian Nesbitt 1
Two Royal Saints—Fr. Hilarion, O.F.M. 1
New Life—Fr. Kilian Hennrich, O.F.M. Cap. 1
Readings on the Third Order Rule—Fr. Forest McGee,
   O.F.M. 1
The Christian Home—Fr. Celestine, O.F.M. 2
The Invincible Prefect—Fr. Theodosius, O.F.M. Cap 2
Franciscan Legends, 2 Series—Mary J. Malloy ..... Each .1
Galilee of Francis—Marie Donegan Walsh 1
Glories of the Franciscan Order—Fr. Francis B. Steck,
   O.F.M. 1
St. Francis of Assisi—The Poverello—L. S. Kenny 1
Rome Hath Spoken—Papal Pronouncements 5
Maggie—Fr. Marion Habig, O.F.M., Cloth 1.2
                                  Paper 8
The Seraphic Highway—Fr. Fulgence Meyer, O.F.M. 1.0
A Layman's Order—Fr. Juvenal, O.F.M. 0
A Call and the Answer—Fr. James, O.F.M. 0
Key to Happiness—Fr. Basil, O.F.M. Cap 0
What's Your Objection? (to Third Order) .... .01

POSTAGE EXTRA

FRANCISCAN HERALD PRESS
1434 West 51st Street
Chicago, Illinois